EARTHWISE

Weather

Jim Pipe

Franklin Watts
London • Sydney

CONTENTS

© Aladdin Books Ltd 2004

Designed and produced by
Aladdin Books Ltd
28 Percy Street
London W1T 2BZ

First published in
Great Britain in 2004 by
Franklin Watts
96 Leonard Street
London EC2A 4XD

Design
Flick, Book Design
and Graphics

Educational Consultant
Jackie Holderness

Picture research
Brian Hunter Smart

ISBN 0 7496 5398 1

A catalogue record for
this book is available
from the British Library.

Printed in UAE

All rights reserved

INTRODUCTION

Whenever we say "it's raining" or "it's sunny", we are talking about the weather. It affects our lives every day, from the clothes we wear and the food we eat, to the way we travel. Good or bad weather can even change how we feel!

HOW TO USE THIS BOOK

Look for the symbol of the magnifying glass for tips and ideas on how to watch the weather.

The paintbrush boxes contain an activity you can do that is related to the weather.

WHAT IS WEATHER?

Weather is what is happening in the atmosphere, the thick blanket of air that surrounds the Earth.

It tells us how hot or cold it is, how wet or dry it is, how cloudy it is or how hard the wind is blowing. Because weather is always on the move, it is always changing!

The planets Venus, Mars, Saturn, Jupiter, Uranus and Neptune all have weather too, though their atmospheres are made up of poisonous gases rather than air. In 1989, the spacecraft Voyager 2 took pictures of an enormous hurricane on the surface of Neptune (below).

What we wear (below) often depends on the weather.

Rainbows are a sign of changing weather. They are caused by sunlight shining through raindrops.

Weather Words

What weather do you like best? Think about some words you could use to describe your favourite weather, then write a poem or a story about it. You could also interview some friends to see which kind of weather they like best.

damp   breezy   calm
stormy   fresh   bright
sunny   cloudy

Bad weather brings all sorts of problems. Farmers need sunshine and rain for a good harvest (left), but too much rain or sunshine can also destroy their crops.

Snow (left), ice and fog can make driving dangerous and cause delays at airports. Strong winds can cause power cuts and knock down trees. Every year hurricanes and tornadoes destroy hundreds of buildings and kill many people.

CLIMATE

If we say "it's always sunny here", we are talking about climate. Climate refers to how the weather behaves over many years. The climate of a place depends on how near it is to the equator, how far it is from the sea (right) or how high up the place is. The Earth has many different landscapes, all with very different climates.

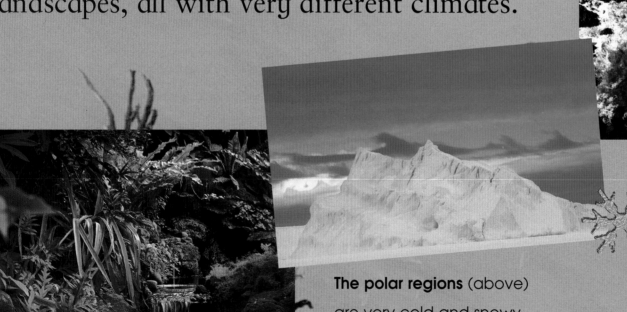

The polar regions (above) are very cold and snowy.

In **tropical rainforests** (left), near the equator, it is hot and rainy all year.

Deserts are hot, dry and dusty (below).

Holiday Destinations

Snowy mountain regions are a great place to ski.

Many people like to go on holiday to places with a hot climate, such as Florida or the Canary Islands. Can you find where these are on a map? Are they close to the equator?

If you could go on holiday anywhere in the world, where would you go? Find out about the climate of the place from books, the internet or CD-ROMS. What is the weather like there compared to where you live?

Many resorts are by the sea as water sports are great fun in the Sun!

Florida is a popular resort because it is sunny for much of the year.

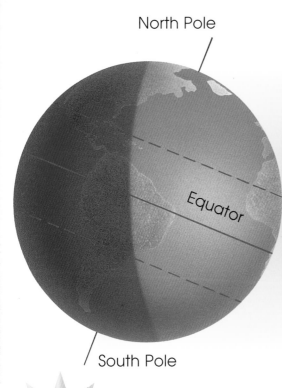

North Pole

Equator

South Pole

THE SUN

Believe it or not, the Sun causes all of our weather. Due to the tilt of our planet, the Sun heats up places near the equator much more than places near the poles (left).

The different hot and cold regions on Earth constantly heat and cool the air around our planet. This causes the air to move – the wind – and turns water in the air into clouds, rain and snow.

SCORCHER!

Most people love a hot, sunny day but we have to be careful – the same rays that warm up our planet can also burn our skin.

Between 10 am and 4 pm, when the Sun is highest in the sky, it is best to be in the shade. If you are out in the Sun, protect your skin with Sun lotion and wear a hat!

Most parts of the world have regular changes in weather that we call seasons. That's because at different times of year, different parts of the Earth are closer to the Sun. In summer, your area is closest to the Sun, which is why it is the hottest part of the year.

Sunny Scenes

The world looks very different when the Sun is out. You can see for yourself if you draw or paint two pictures of the same place, one when it is cloudy and one on a sunny day. Look at the differences. Do colours look brighter in the Sun? Are there more shadows? You may find that some animals like the Sun, while others like the shade.

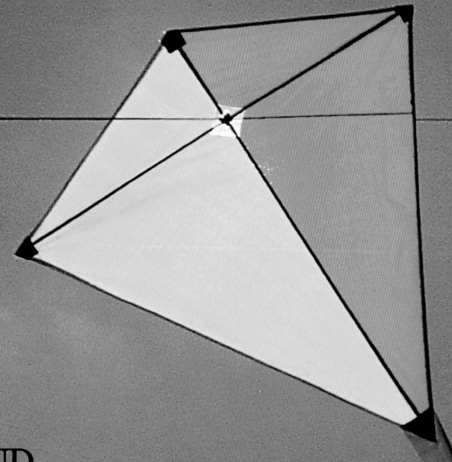

The power of the wind pushes kites up into the air.

WIND

Wind is moving air. You cannot see it, but you can often hear it. It can blow so gently that you can hardly feel it or it can blow so hard that it knocks buildings over.

Winds carry warmth and coolness around the world. They create changes in the weather. A cold wind can make a hot day cool and a warm wind can melt the snow. A wind can bring rain, or it can blow the rainclouds away.

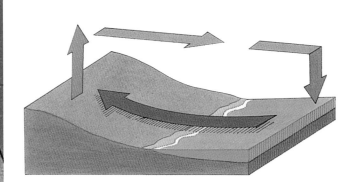

Wind is caused by the Sun heating some parts of the Earth more than others. The air above these areas warms up, too, and begins to rise. Then cooler air flows in to take its place (left). The movement of this hot and cold air from one place to another is what we call wind.

Birds and insects use the wind to help them move about. Plants also use the wind to help scatter their seeds. Sycamore seeds (left) grow in pairs and have flat, thin wings that make them whirl in the wind. A lime tree seed has a winged case so that it floats in the air as it falls to the ground (below).

Dandelion seeds have feathery parachutes and may be carried a long way on the wind. Puff on a dandelion and see how far the seeds travel (left).

WATER IN THE AIR

Even on a clear sunny day, places far away can look hazy. This is mostly because of water in the air. The warmth of the Sun heats the water in oceans, rivers and lakes. The water evaporates, or becomes an invisible gas, called water vapour. We know it's there because when it gets cold, the vapour turns back into water or ice, causing dewdrops, clouds, rain or snow.

High up in the air, it is very cold, and the wings of airplanes can become coated with ice. To avoid this, planes use heat from their engines to melt the ice while they are flying. Once planes are back on the ground, chemicals are also used to melt the ice.

You have probably noticed that it usually gets colder at night. As the air cools down, water vapour in the air turns back into water, in a process known as condensation. This water might make the grass wet with dew, even when it has not been raining.

F ROST

On a very cold night, often when the sky is clear, dewdrops turn to ice. This is frost, a thin layer of ice covering grass, leaves and other surfaces outdoors. Frost can also create beautiful patterns on a window.

Jack Frost

In some parts of the world, frosty nights are linked with Jack Frost, an elf-like character who leaves his icy finger marks on the window. Imagine what Jack Frost looks like – can you paint a picture of him?

WHAT ARE CLOUDS?

Clouds are made up of millions of droplets of water or ice that are so light that they can float in the air. Clouds form when warm air rises high into the sky and cools down. As the water vapour in the air cools, it turns into tiny droplets of water or ice. When these droplets gather together (above left), a cloud is born!

STEAM • CLOUDS

The white puffs of smoke from a steam train are also made up of tiny droplets of water. These clouds form when boiling hot water vapour from inside the engine, called steam, meets the cold air outside. When you boil water in a kettle, the same white vapour appears from the spout.

Fog is the name for clouds that form close to the ground or near to the surface of the sea. It often appears early in the morning after a calm, clear night and disappears as the day warms up. Driving or sailing is dangerous when there is thick fog (right), as it makes it impossible to see very far. Thin, hazy fog is also known as mist.

Dreamy

Sad

Happy

Light

Stormy

Stormy Feelings

When you look at clouds, how do you feel – dreamy or sad, happy or lonely? Clouds often suggest different emotions, so they appear in lots of songs and poems. Listen out for songs that mention clouds, storms or rain. Then write your own story, song or poem, using clouds to describe your feelings.

CLOUDY SKIES

You may have noticed that some clouds look white in the sunshine, while other clouds are grey – they are so thick that light from the Sun cannot pass through them. But the colour, shape and height of clouds can all provide clues to the weather in the next few hours or days.

CLOUD • NAMES

There are three main groups of clouds. Cirrus are wispy clouds that appear high in the sky. Cumulus are the fluffy white clouds you often see on a sunny day. Stratus clouds are the smooth sheets of grey cloud that stay close to the ground and usually bring rain or drizzle.

Cirrus means "curl of hair", cumulus means "heap" and stratus means "layer". Can you see how they got their names?

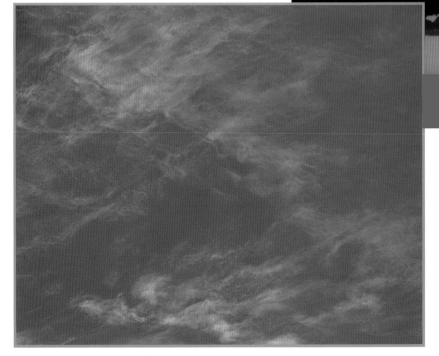

Cirrus clouds (above) are made of ice crystals.

In summer, giant cumulonimbus clouds often bring thunderstorms. The fast moving air inside these clouds makes drops of water and ice rub against each other. This creates lightning, which is like an enormous spark of electricity. When lightning flashes, it also makes the hot air around it explode with a crash of thunder.

If you watch cumulus clouds (right) on a sunny day, you can see that they are always changing shape. This happens because when a cloud meets drier, warmer air, parts of the cloud turn back into invisible water vapour, and vanish!

RAIN

Rain is water that falls in drops from the sky. It happens when tiny droplets of water in the clouds join together to make bigger and bigger drops. Finally, the water drops get too heavy to float in the air, so they fall to the ground as rain.

Rain is a very important source of fresh water. In many hot countries, people collect rainwater in containers so there is a supply of fresh water during the dry season.

How are these girls keeping dry in the rain?

Umbrellas

Waterproof

Rubber boots

Plip Plop Pitter Patter

Splish

Splash Splosh

Raindrops can be big or small, and the bigger they are, the faster they fall! Small raindrops, known as drizzle, often fall from low clouds. Drizzle falls so slowly it seems to wrap itself around you.

In a summer storm, you can be quickly soaked by huge drops of rain in a shower that lasts for just a few minutes. Watch how hard these big drops hit the ground. Other clouds give off a steady stream of rain that lasts for several hours.

S TEAMED UP

After a hot shower, the air in a bathroom is warm and wet. When this warm, wet air meets a cold mirror, water drops, known as "condensation", form on the surface of the mirror.

Rain Sounds

The sound that rain makes depends on whether it is heavy or light and what it is falling on. What words would you use for the sound of rain? Next time it rains, have a listen and make up some of your own!

SNOW

In very cold weather, snow can fall from the same grey clouds that usually bring rain, covering the ground with a blanket of snow. Strong winds pile the snow up on the sides of roads (below) and against walls, creating snowdrifts.

Playing in the snow (left)

S NOWFLAKES

Every snowflake has six sides, but no one has ever found two that are exactly the same! That's because a snowflake is made up of tiny ice crystals. As many as 100 ice crystals may cling together to form a snowflake about 2.5 centimetres across.

The heaviest snowfalls are on mountain ranges such as the Rocky Mountains in North America and the Alps in Europe (left). Many mountains have snow on their upper slopes all year round. Sometimes, a huge block of snow tumbles down the side of a mountain. This falling snow, called an avalanche, can travel at speeds of over 160 kilometres per hour.

Snow falls when the air is below freezing, so the water vapour in clouds turns into tiny ice crystals. As the ice crystals fall, they bump into each other and stick together to form snowflakes.

Sleet occurs when melted snow crystals or raindrops fall through cold air and freeze into tiny lumps of clear ice.

Hailstones (above) are hard lumps of ice that usually form in thunderstorms. Big hailstones are the size of oranges and can easily break windows or dent cars.

STORMS

A **hurricane** (above) is a powerful storm that may be hundreds of kilometres wide. Its swirling winds can blow at speeds of up to 320 kilometres per hour. Hurricanes often cause floods and can do more damage than any other kind of weather.

A storm usually brings very strong winds, called gales, which are often accompanied by other bad weather such as heavy rains or snowfalls.

Small storms may last just a few hours and do very little damage. The largest storms can last for weeks. They can uproot trees, blow away small buildings, or create floods that sweep away crops, houses and cars.

A blizzard (left) is a heavy fall of snow combined with strong, cold winds. They can pile up huge snowdrifts, making it very hard for people or cars to move around.
A dust devil (right) is a like a mini tornado. Found mostly in deserts, it can suck sand and dust 300 metres or more above the ground.

A **tornado** is a whirlwind that forms below a thunderstorm. It looks like a dark funnel of cloud (left). Tornado winds spin around at speeds of over 480 kilometres per hour, which is why they are also called "twisters".

Tornadoes can cause terrible damage – knocking aside big trees and picking up lorries, cattle and even mobile homes. But most are much weaker and last only a few minutes.

Sometimes the wind sends giant clouds of sand or dust racing across the desert. This cloud, called a **sandstorm,** is so rough it can rub the paint off cars in just a few hours. High in the sky, winds can carry sand for thousands of kilometres, turning rain or snow pink in countries far away!

LIVING WITH WEATHER

Over thousands of years, animals and plants have developed ways of life suited to every climate. People have also learned to survive in many climates. We can wear clothes or live in buildings suited to hot or cold weather. We can also travel across most landscapes (left).

ANIMAL TACTICS

Next time you visit a wildlife park, see if you can spot which animals are suited to hot or cold climates. For example, polar bears have thick fur and thick layers of fat to keep them warm in the icy polar regions where they live. Meerkats are furry too, but they avoid the hot sun of their southern African home by staying in their burrow.

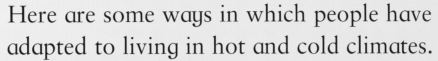

Here are some ways in which people have adapted to living in hot and cold climates.

Living in a Hot Climate

This family in India are wearing loose, light clothes to keep cool in hot weather.

This house in Africa provides shade in the heat. Many houses in very hot regions also have shutters. People close them during the day to keep the hot air out and open them at night to let the cool air in.

Living in a Cold Climate

Houses in cold climates tend to be built of solid, heavy materials such as brick or stone, so they won't blow away. The walls are thick to keep the heat in, and sloping roofs allow snow to slide to the ground.

This family live high up in the Andes mountains in Peru. They wear many layers of thick clothing and warm hats to keep out the cold.

WEATHER WATCHING

Knowing what the weather is going to be like is an important part of planning our lives. To find out, most people listen to the weather forecast. This tells them their daily and weekly weather and gives warnings of severe weather such as storms or tornadoes.

1 Weather stations all over the world collect information such as wind speed, temperature and rainfall. Many of these stations are on land, others are on ships or on drifting buoys at sea.

2 Up in the sky, weather balloons (left) and planes also take measurements, while weather satellites in space beam back pictures of cloud and temperature patterns (top).

3 All this information is fed into computers (far left) to create weather maps. Using these, forecasters can work out what the weather will be like for the next few days.

A Weather Diary

Checking a pine cone

Check the sky each day to see whether it is sunny or cloudy or if rain is on the way. A pine cone can help (right) – it opens up when the weather is dry, and closes up again before it rains. If you have something with long streamers on, take it outside: the more it flaps, the windier it is! Use a large plastic bottle to make a rain gauge (bottom right). Cut the top off with scissors and wedge it upside down in the bottom half. When it rains, check how much water trickles into the bottom.

Waves grow larger when it is windy (above).

Testing the wind

Rain gauge

OUR CHANGING WEATHER

We now understand a lot about how weather works, but it is still very hard to forecast, especially as the weather on our planet is constantly changing. So when you get up in the morning, it's still best to look outside and check!

Lots of activities are best in the Sun!

Anyone who works outdoors watches the weather closely.

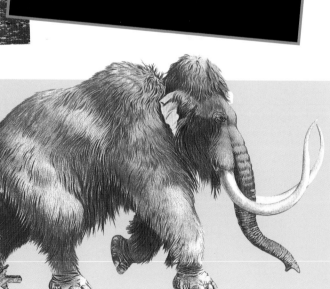
Bad weather can make travel slow or unsafe.

The world's weather and climate have never stopped changing. For example, around 20,000 years ago, a third of the Earth was covered in ice over 240m thick! Many of the creatures living then had woolly coats to keep them warm, such as woolly mammoths and rhinoceroses.

In the past 30 years, the world's weather has become warmer, partly due to the gases from factories (left), rubbish dumps and fires polluting the atmosphere. Scientists aren't sure what will happen if the world keeps getting warmer, but recent years have seen a rise in storms and floods (top).

YOU CAN HELP

There are laws in many countries to control the amount of smoke and pollution from factories and homes. However, we can all help by using less energy in our daily lives. Why not try cycling or walking to school instead of taking a car and remember to switch off lights when you aren't using them.

USEFUL WORDS

air – the mixture of gases that surrounds the Earth.

atmosphere – the mixture of gases that surrounds any planet. It is usually made up of several layers.

climate – the usual pattern of weather that a place has over many years.

condensation – when warm water vapour meets a cold surface it turns back into drops of liquid, called condensation.

equator – an imaginary circle around the middle of the Earth, halfway between the North pole and the South pole.

evaporation – when a liquid such as water is heated and turns into a gas, it evaporates.

forecast – to tell what is coming; to use observations to predict something in the future, such as the weather.

freeze – to turn into ice. Water becomes ice when it freezes.

poles – the ends of the Earth. One pole is in the far north of our planet, the other in the far south.

pollute – to make something dirty with waste or chemicals.

rain gauge – an instrument for measuring rainfall.

seasons – regular changes in temperature and weather that happen every year at about the same time.

storm - violent bad weather.

temperature – how hot or cold something is, usually measured in degrees of centigrade or fahrenheit.

thunderstorm – a storm that produces thunder and lightning.

water vapour – the name for water when it is a gas. Hot water vapour is known as steam.

Find out more

If you want to find out more, take a look at these books and websites:

Books: Focus On Weather (Franklin Watts); Discovering Nature - Weather (Franklin Watts); Horrible Geography: Stormy Weather (Scholastic).

Websites: www.weatherandkids.co; www.miamisci.org/hurricane; www.wxdude.co; www.ecokids.ca

RAINBOWS

When white sunlight passes through a raindrop, the water splits it into red, orange, yellow, green, blue, indigo and violet, creating a rainbow.

You can sometimes see small rainbows appear in the spray from the sea, a waterfall or a garden hose.

INDEX

Photocredits
Abbreviations: l-left, r-right, b-bottom, t-top, c-centre, m-middle
Front cover tl, tr & br, back cover, 1, 4-5, 6br, 8tl, 8c, 8tr, 9tr, 9bl, 10b, 14tl, 15tr, 15bl, 16br, 17tl, 18br, 20br, 24 both, 25t, 26tr, 26bl, 28mr, 29tr, 31bl, 32b — Corbis. Front cover mr, 7, 10mr, 11mr, 17br, 18-19, 21tl, 28ml, 30-31 — Digital Stock. Front cover inset, 4bl, 13br, 18bl, 19mr, 27tr, 27bm — Flick Smith. 2-3, 5bl, 8-9, 12-13, 14-15, 20tl, 21mr, 25bl, 27bl, 29tl — Photodisc. 3b — PBD. 4mr, 5ml — Stockbyte. 5tr, 7br, 29br — Brand X Pictures. 8bl, 12bl — Comstock. 9br, 10tl, 11c, 11br, 18mr — Corel. 11tl — Flat Earth. 14br — Julian Cox. 22-23 — Corbis Royalty Free. 23bl, 30tr — Digital Vision. 26bm — Ramon Preciado/U.S. Navy. 28tr — Roger Vlitos,